LEADERS LIKE US

YURI KOCHIYAMA

ROURKE'S
SCHOOL to HOME
CONNECTIONS

BEFORE AND DURING READING ACTIVITIES

Before Reading: *Building Background Knowledge and Vocabulary*

Building background knowledge can help children process new information and build upon what they already know. Before reading a book, it is important to tap into what children already know about the topic. This will help them develop their vocabulary and increase their reading comprehension.

Questions and Activities to Build Background Knowledge:

1. Look at the front cover of the book and read the title. What do you think this book will be about?
2. What do you already know about this topic?
3. Take a book walk and skim the pages. Look at the table of contents, photographs, captions, and bold words. Did these text features give you any information or predictions about what you will read in this book?

Vocabulary: *Vocabulary Is Key to Reading Comprehension*

Use the following directions to prompt a conversation about each word.

- Read the vocabulary words.
- What comes to mind when you see each word?
- What do you think each word means?

Vocabulary Words:

- *activists*
- *civil disobedience*
- *FBI*
- *incarceration*
- *injustices*
- *leave*
- *legacy*
- *lifeline*

During Reading: *Reading for Meaning and Understanding*

To achieve deep comprehension of a book, children are encouraged to use close reading strategies. During reading, it is important to have children stop and make connections. These connections result in deeper analysis and understanding of a book.

Close Reading a Text

During reading, have children stop and talk about the following:

- Any confusing parts
- Any unknown words
- Text to text, text to self, text to world connections
- The main idea in each chapter or heading

Encourage children to use context clues to determine the meaning of any unknown words. These strategies will help children learn to analyze the text more thoroughly as they read.

When you are finished reading this book, turn to the next-to-last page for **Text-Dependent Questions** and an **Extension Activity**.

TABLE OF CONTENTS

LETTER WRITER

Have you ever felt alone?
Did you need to know someone was thinking of you?
Yuri Kochiyama might have written you a letter.

Way past midnight, while everyone else is sleeping, Yuri writes letters at the kitchen table. She writes to friends, **activists**, and political prisoners. Yuri knows a letter can be a **lifeline**. People need to know someone is on their side.

Mary Yuriko Nakahara, later known as Yuri, was born on May 19, 1921. She had an "all-American" childhood in San Pedro, California. She was very social and active in sports and community service.

Yuri finished junior college ready to start working. She worked as a Sunday school teacher, in a department store, and volunteered with the Women's Ambulance and Defense Corps of America. This group helped during World War II (WWII) with first aid and other war efforts.

W A
A
D C
W A
A
D C

Yuri's world changed on Decenber 7, 1941 when Pearl Harbor was bombed by Japan. Within hours, the **FBI** came to arrest Yuri's father, Mr. Seiichi Nakahara, who she called Pop. He was sick when they came. Still, he was taken away in his bathrobe and slippers.

Japanese American community leaders were being arrested just for being Japanese. Pop was released after six weeks. He had done nothing wrong. But they hadn't treated his illness. Twelve hours after returning home, Pop died at the young age of 56.

Shortly after Pop's death, Yuri and the rest of her family were also sent away. Yuri, her mother, older brother Art, and twin brother Pete, were put in an **incarceration** camp in Jerome, Arkansas for two years.

JAPANESE AMERICAN INCARCERATION

During WWII, 120,000 Japanese Americans on the west coast had to leave their homes and go to ten incarceration camps. They were called enemies and imprisoned because of their Japanese descent. The US was fighting against Germany too, but German Americans didn't receive the same treatment. After the war, this was found to be wrong and based on racism.

BECOMING AN ACTIVIST

Yuri met Bill Kochiyama when he was on **leave** from the army. She and Bill had a wartime romance through letters. Yuri also started a group called the "Crusaders." They wrote letters to Japanese American soldiers to let them know they were not alone. They wrote to 13,000 soldiers!

After the war, Yuri and Bill got married in New York City. They didn't have much money and lived in Harlem's Manhattanville. Manhattanville was a housing project; homes the government helped pay for that didn't cost much. They raised their six children there.

In Harlem, Yuri became an activist. She started her fight against inequality and other **injustices**. She joined her Puerto Rican and Black neighbors fighting for safe streets and better schools for their children. She learned about **civil disobedience** as a way to protest.

When Yuri saw injustice, she couldn't hold back...

...she marched in protests with her family...

and even got arrested twice!

Yuri was part of many organizations that focused on the causes she cared about. She supported political prisoners. She fought to seek justice for the wrongful incarceration of Japanese Americans during WWII. Around this time is when she decided to stop using the name Mary and go by her Japanese name, Yuri.

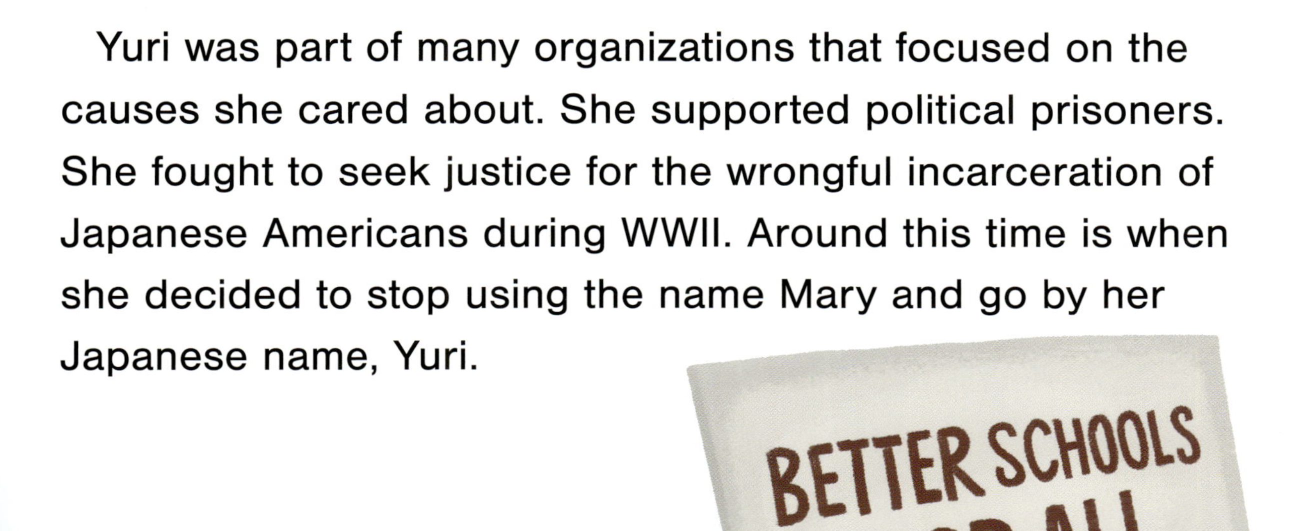

SUPPORTING POLITICAL PRISONERS
Yuri experienced being wrongly imprisoned. She knew how it felt. So she stood up for people who were put in prison for their political beliefs

Yuri and Bill's apartment became known as "Grand Central Station." Like the railway station, people from all across the country and world visited. They shared ideas for a better world. Visitors included *hibakusha*, a Japanese name given to survivors of the atomic bomb, Malcolm X, and countless others.

BUILDING THE TOGETHERNESS OF ALL PEOPLES

Some of Yuri's activism put her in the spotlight. When Malcolm X was shot, Yuri ran to comfort him as he was dying. Yuri was also arrested at the Statue of Liberty. She was protesting for Puerto Rican independence. But some of her most important work was behind the scenes. While she worked as a waitress, she also acted as a message center. Activists would leave messages with Yuri and Yuri would deliver them.

To Yuri, building what she called the "togetherness of all peoples" was key. She wanted to bring people of different racial and ethnic groups, generations, and all kinds of backgrounds together. Many say it is her strongest lasting **legacy**.

PUERTO RICAN INDEPENDENCE

Yuri joined protesters who put the Puerto Rican flag on the Statue of Liberty's crown. It was a call for the island's independence. Though Puerto Ricans are US citizens, they cannot vote in Presidential elections and have limited rights.

Yuri was honored for her work as an activist. She was one of 25 people recognized for their work for the Harlem community. She was one of 1,000 women nominated for a collective Nobel Prize in 2005.

She was honored by individuals and friends with gifts of teddy bears. She cherished her "K Bear" (Kochiyama Bear) collection. Each one was special to her because it was from a different special person.

Yuri wrote a memoir titled *Passing It On*. She did it mainly for her "Grands," or grandchildren. In 1999, Yuri moved to Oakland, California to live closer to her children. She continued to support activist movements until she died in 2014.

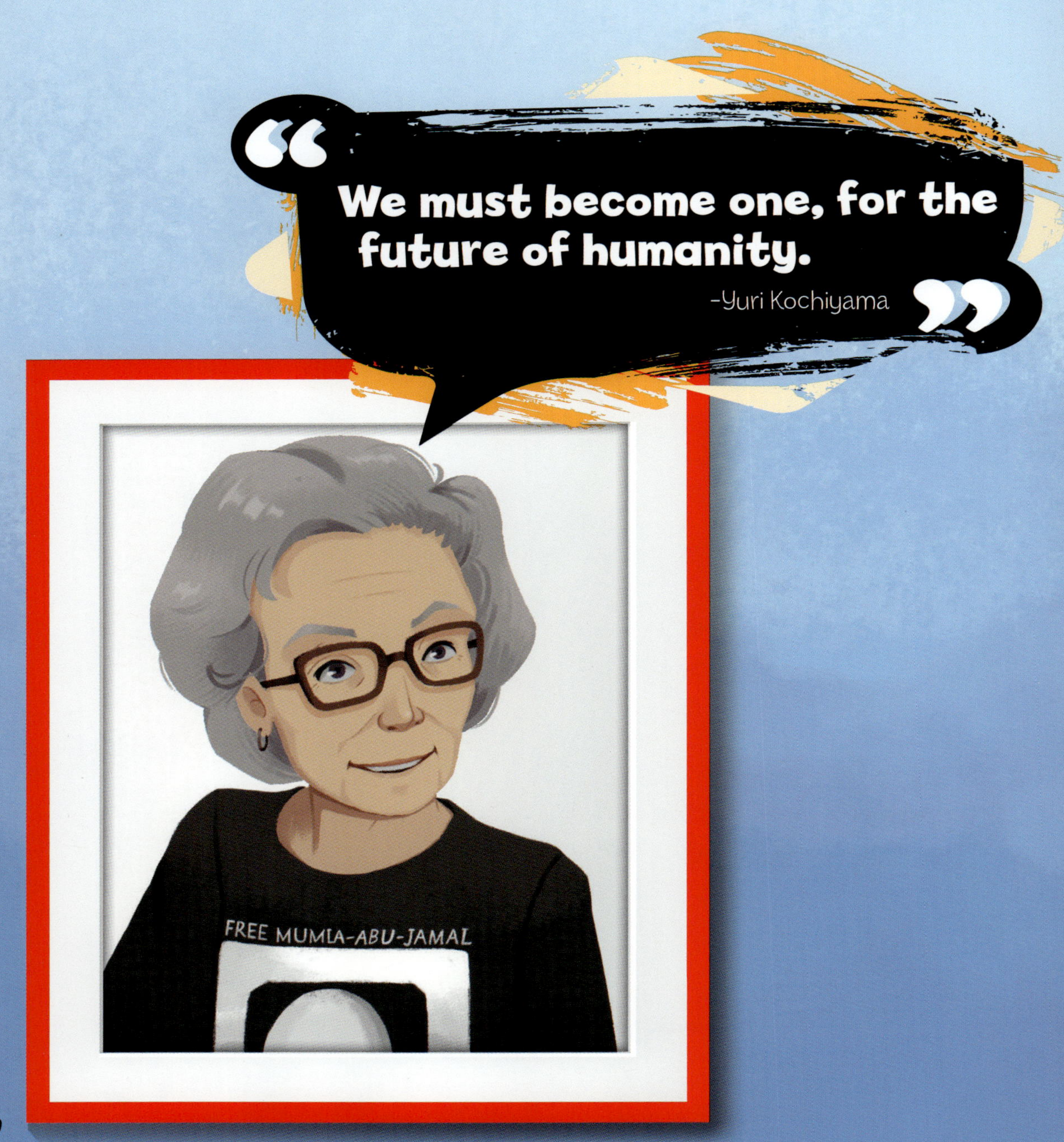

TIME LINE

1921	Mary Yuriko Nakahara is born on May 19 in San Pedro, California to Tsuyako and Seiichi Nakara.
1941	Yuri graduates from Compton Junior College.
1941	Yuri's father is arrested by the FBI on December 7 after Pearl Harbor is bombed.
1942	Yuri's father is released on January 20, but dies the next day.
1942	Yuri and her family are sent to the Santa Anita Assembly Center, then to an incarceration camp in Jerome, Arkansas, until 1944.
1946	Yuri moves to New York City and marries Bill Kochiyama.
1963	Yuri is arrested at a protest against unfair hiring practices. It leads to her meeting Malcolm X and befriending him until his death on February 21, 1969.
1964	Malcolm X meets *hibakusha* guests from Japan at Yuri's home on June 6.
1977	Yuri is arrested at the Statue of Liberty with 29 other protesters for Puerto Rican independence.
1988	The Civil Liberties Act passes which provides an official apology for the Japanese American incarceration and compensation for survivors.
1993	Bill Kochiyama dies of heart complications on October 25.
2004	Yuri's memoir, *Passing It On*, is published.
2005	Yuri is included among 1,000 women collectively nominated for the Nobel Prize.
2014	Yuri dies on June 1 in Berkeley, California, of natural causes at 93.

GLOSSARY

activists (ak-TIV-ists): people who take actions to create change

civil disobedience (SIV-uhl dis-uh-BEE-dee-uhns): a way to peacefully protest by breaking a law to protest a wrong

FBI (eff-bee-eye): the Federal Bureau of Investigation, a government office that is in charge of the country's security

incarceration (in-KAR-sur-aye-shuhn): the state of being in prison

injustices (in-JUHS-tis-is): unfairness or situations that lack justice

leave (leev): time away from work or military service

legacy (LEG-uh-see): something valuable that's passed down from one generation to another

lifeline (life-line): something that can save someone's life

INDEX

TEXT-DEPENDENT QUESTIONS

1. Why was writing letters so important to Yuri?
2. What happened to Yuri's father and her family after Pearl Harbor was bombed?
3. Where did Yuri and Bill live after they got married?
4. What were some of the causes Yuri supported as an activist?
5. What are some of the ways Yuri's activism has been honored?

EXTENSION ACTIVITY

Think of someone you would like to create a stronger connection with. Write a letter to that person and consider becoming pen pals. It can be someone who lives near or far. Talk with a trusted adult in your life to decide who to write to. Write your letter with pen and paper and use an envelope and a stamp to mail it!

ABOUT THE AUTHOR

Karen Su is a professor of Global Asian Studies at the University of Illinois Chicago. She teaches college students about activists like Yuri Kochiyama to inspire them to become involved in activism for causes that are important to them. She wants readers to get involved in whatever way is possible for them, even if it's behind the scenes. All actions will make a difference for the future of humanity.

ABOUT THE ILLUSTRATOR

Arlo Li is an illustrator originally from China and now based in the US. He enjoys creating bright, whimsical, and colorful illustrations and specializes in children's books. He seeks to tell stories through his work and uses tiny details to bring those stories to life. He loves bringing his unique artistic vision to every project he works on.

www.rourkebooks.com

Quote source: Diane Carol Fujino. *Heartbeat of Struggle: The Revolutionary Life of Yuri Kochiyama,* University of Minnesota Press, 2005, p. 301
Edited by: Hailey Scragg
Illustrations by: Arlo Li
Cover and interior layout by: J.J. Giddings

Library of Congress PCN Data

Yuri Kochiyama / Karen Su
(Leaders Like Us)
ISBN 978-1-73165-728-2 (hard cover)
ISBN 978-1-73165-715-2 (soft cover)
ISBN 978-1-73165-741-1(e-book)
ISBN 978-1-73165-754-1 (e-pub)
Library of Congress Control Number: 2023933042

Rourke Educational Media
Printed in the United States of America
01-1982311937